Between You & me God

Prayers by Catholic Kids

Compiled and Edited by Diane M. Lynch

Pauline
BOOKS & MEDIA
Boston

Nihil Obstat:
Rev. Thomas W. Buckley, S.T.D., S.S.L.

Imprimatur:
✠Seán Cardinal O'Malley, O.F.M. Cap.
Archbishop of Boston
April 7, 2008

Library of Congress Cataloging-in-Publication Data
Between you & me, God : prayers by Catholic kids / compiled and edited by
Diane M. Lynch.
    p. cm.
  ISBN 0-8198-1171-8 (pbk.)
  1. Catholic children--Prayers and devotions. 2. Catholic Church--Prayers and
devotions--Juvenile literature. I. Title: Between you and me, God. II. Lynch,
Diane M., date.
  BX2150.B44 2008
  242'.82--dc22

2008009321

The English translation of the Act of Contrition from *Rite of Penance* © 1974,
International Committee on English in the Liturgy, Inc. (ICEL); the English
translation of the Angelus and the Prayer for the Dead from *A Book of Prayers*
© 1982, ICEL. All rights reserved.

English translation of the Apostles' Creed and Doxology by the International
Consultation on English Texts (ICET).

Cover design by Mary Joseph Peterson, FSP

Published by Pauline Books & Media, 50 Saint Pauls Avenue, Boston, MA
02130-3491

Printed in U.S.A.

www.pauline.org

Pauline Books & Media is the publishing house of the Daughters of St. Paul,
an international congregation of women religious serving the Church with the
communications media.

1 2 3 4 5 6 7 8 9   11 10 09 08

Why Do We Pray? And How? / 8

Part One:
Prayers about Everyday Life

CONTENTS

Part Two:
Prayers to Favorite Saints

Part Three:
Traditional Catholic Prayers

Why Do We Pray? And How?

"I don't know how to pray."

Lots of people say that—both kids and adults.

There are many ways to pray, but, basically, all prayer is spending time talking with God. Just as our family and friends like it when we hang out with them, God really likes us to spend time with him, too.

One kind of praying is the kind we do together in church, as in the celebration of the Eucharist. This is called the Liturgy. It's the prayer of the whole Church, and we all pray together in the same way and at the same time.

Another kind of prayer is when we take time to be alone with God. We can say anything we like. We don't have to use prayers written by someone else, but sometimes they can help us get started.

We can tell God everything. He knows us inside and out, so nothing will surprise him or shock him. He knows what we're thinking and feeling, but he really likes us to talk to him about it. Why? Because God loves us more than all our family and friends put together.

He's our heavenly Father. And Jesus is the Son of God, who became a man and gave his life for us out of love.

Prayer is something that's so important, we should do it every day.

One way to pray every day is to take a little time before you go to bed. First tell God about all the good things that happened that day. Say thank you! Then think of the things that weren't so good. Ask him to help you deal with any difficult issues. Tell him you're sorry for whatever you did that was wrong. It only takes a few minutes.

This book is full of prayers written and prayed by kids your age. There's a section of traditional Catholic prayers, too. You can use any of the prayers to help you get started talking to God. Tell him what you're worrying about, wondering about, feeling happy about, or whatever. Just pray. The best time to do it is…right now!

Maria Grace Dateno, FSP

PRAYERS ABOUT
EVERYDAY LIFE

PART ONE

Introduction

These prayers have been written by kids between the ages of ten and thirteen. They come from all over the United States and Canada. They live in cities, in suburbs, and in rural communities. Some of them attend Catholic schools, some go to public schools, and some are home schooled. What do they all have in common?

All of them want to talk with God about their lives—and to listen to him, too. There are lots of different ways to pray, with or without words. There's no wrong way to pray.

You may find prayers in this section you can relate to. The more you think about them, the easier it will be for you to speak to God from your own heart. Remember, he's always listening!

ANIMALS

Prayer for Pets

My Lord,

Please look after all lost pets. Help pets who have wandered away from home to find their way back to their loved ones. Help abandoned pets find new, loving families. Help me take care of my own pets. Please let them be happy, healthy, and friendly. Please take care of all the stray animals. Amen.

— Tucker, age 11

13

Prayer for Shadow

Dear God,

A while ago we had to put my dog, Shadow, to sleep. She was really old and really sick. I cried and cried because it was so sad. I know we couldn't let her suffer, but I miss her a lot. God, I know you love dogs, too, because you created them and you love everything you created. Thank you for all the fun I had with Shadow, and I hope I get another dog someday. Love,

— Taylor, age 12

For All the Animals

Dear God,

I pray for all the animals that are sick or suffering in the world. I hope that endangered species like giant pandas and crocodiles survive and soon won't be endangered anymore.

— Sara, age 10

15

ASKING BLESSINGS FOR OTHERS

For Everyone Who Is Disabled and for Their Families

Dear Almighty Father,

I would like to pray for all the disabled people in the world, especially for my brother who was diagnosed with autism when he was four years old. It is a big responsibility to be related to someone who is disabled. Give strength to all the autistic people of the world and help them to get a good education. I pray for everyone who is disabled and for their families.

— *Alan, age 12*

Your Loving Hands

Dear Lord,

Now that we are approaching cold weather and nights will soon be freezing, please watch over those who don't have shelter or a warm place to stay. Keep them in your loving hands. Amen.

— *Carol, age 13*

17

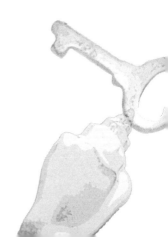

Lord, Bless the Mentally Disabled Kids

Dear God,

Please bless all the kids with mental disabilities. Please make sure they don't get taken advantage of and that they have the courage to stick up for themselves. And please bless and help their parents to have the patience to help their children and not to give up on them. Amen.

— *Megan, age 12*

18

A Special Place in Your Heart

Dear God,

I want to ask you to keep in mind the poor and the disabled. One of the Sisters in our school visited a home for the blind in the Philippines. She showed us a slideshow of the children who live there. And that's when it hit me: I realized how very fortunate I am. So I would like to thank you for what I have, but also I would like you to keep those who are less fortunate in a special place in your heart. Amen.

— Zachary, age 12

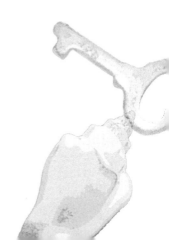

EVERYDAY

A Loving Set of Arms

Dear God,

Please help the poor children of the world to have a warm place to sleep, meals to eat, and clothes to keep them warm. Send them a loving set of arms to give hugs and kisses to let them know they are loved. Keep them safe and healthy. Amen.

— Anthony, age 11

Becoming More Like Jesus

How We Treat Others

Dear God,
We cannot control what we look like, and
we can't choose what qualities we were born
   with.
Please, O God, help us.
May we not make fun of others because of
   their mental or physical disabilities.
We may not be able to control how others
   behave,
but please help us to have control over our
   own behavior and choices. Amen.

21

— *Dan, age 12*

Dear Jesus

Dear Jesus, help me to be good and to do my chores and schoolwork cheerfully today and every other day. Help me to be pleasing to you in everything I do. Help me to hold my temper when I get mad, and help me to be kind to everyone I meet. Amen.

— Angela, age 10

God, Help Me to Be Better

Dear God,

Help me to be a better person. Help me to always be a good friend and to keep the feelings of others in mind. When I'm rude, please help me to be polite. Please, please help me to be a better sister when I am being mean to my siblings. Help me to do my best at everything I try to do. Amen.

— Sarah, age 11

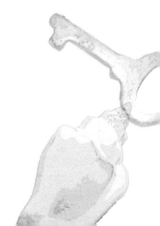

Forgiving Hearts

Jesus, sometimes I get really mad at my sister. She can be so annoying. It feels as though every time I get attention from my parents, she wants even more attention for herself. Sometimes she even makes things up about me and tries to get me in trouble. Please help me to stand up for myself, and also help me to forgive my sister when she does things like that. I will try harder to be nice to her, too. I guess what I am asking is that you help both of us to be forgiving, the way you are. Lord, hear my prayer. Amen.

— *LaShonda, age 10*

Help Me to Be Honest

Almighty God,

Please help me to be honest with myself, my teachers, and with you. Lying is easy, but damaging. It seems like an easy way to get out of problems, but then you get in more trouble and have to lie again. Being honest is hard, but it's a relief, and it's the right thing to do. God, please hear my prayer and help me to be honest. Amen.

—Jordin, age 12

25

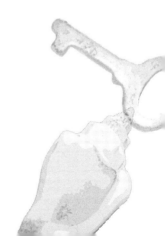

God, I Am So Mad

God, I am so mad at my best friend. He said
some stuff about me that wasn't even true, and
now everyone at school believes it. So now he
says he's sorry, but it's kind of too late. I think
he really is sorry, but it's hard to forgive him.
I know you would have forgiven him, because
you even forgave Judas, which must have been
really difficult. Can you help me to forgive
him? Thanks.

— *Bryan, age 11*

Divorce and Separation

A Pinch of Hurt

Dear Jesus,

In my life, my parents are not together. It's a little tough for me, because I have to switch from place to place. I can feel just a pinch of hurt. But in some places, girls and boys don't have any parents to care for and love them. I ask you to bless all those kids in need of love, care, and shelter, and I ask you to keep them safe. Amen.

— *Resseka, age 10*

27

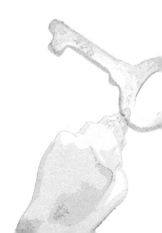

I Miss How It Used to Be

Dear God,

There are many things that I would like to talk to you about, but one thing that is important to me is my family. Over the past year, there have been two divorces in my extended family. This has caused a lot of problems. As time goes on, it just seems to be getting worse. People are not speaking to each other and not inviting each other to family celebrations.

I miss how it used to be, and this is something that is always on my mind. Please guide me to understand this situation and to accept that one day it will all be okay. Amen.

— *Cassandra, age 13*

I Am Hopeful

Dear Jesus,

My family is having a problem. The problem is that my parents are separated. I live with my mom, and I stay with my dad on weekends. More than anything else, I would like my parents to get back together. They are trying really hard and are going to marriage counseling. Please, Jesus, if it is your will, it would be really great if we could all live together and be a family again. My mom says she is feeling hopeful, so I am feeling hopeful, too. Amen.

— Tom, age 11

29

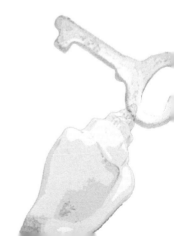

FAITH IN GOD

Help Me to Pray

Dear God,
Please help me to pray.
I often find myself wondering what to say.
I'm unsure of how to talk to you.
I'm very aware of the Our Father and the Hail
Mary, etc., but I want to say more.
When I was younger, I used to talk to you all
   the time.
I found it so easy:
"Dear God, please bless Mommy and Daddy
and Sophia. Bless Grandma-ma and Poppy,
Nana and Papa, and Grandma Suzie. Bless
Mormore and Pa, and Allie, and Jake, and
Natalie, and Kate, and…"
God, help me to find the words I am searching
   for.
Help me to pray. Amen.

— *Rosemary, age 12*

I Love You in So Many Ways

Dear God,

Thank you for giving me this glorious day.
Thanks for my family and friends, whom I love.
Each and every day that passes,
I give thanks to you up above.

The love I receive and give each day
Is something that can't compare
To the love that you give me no matter what,
A love that is always there.

Through Baptism, Eucharist, and
    Confirmation,
I am part of your Church indeed,
A true soldier of Christ in so many ways;
With you by my side I will always succeed.

You always make me feel reassured
When I don't know what to do.
Throughout all my challenges and obstacles,
You are the one who has gotten me through.

I am thankful to you for so many things.
You're important to me every day.
I can't imagine life without you in my heart—
I love and honor you in every way. Amen.

— *Nicole, age 13*

My Hero

Jesus, you guide me every step of the way and lead me in the right direction. I know you're watching down on me from heaven, and you give me the strength to carry on in life. You're my hero because you sacrificed yourself on the cross for us and opened the gates of heaven. You are our Creator and made heaven, earth, and everything on earth. Thank you for always being there for me, and I love you very much.

— Courtney, age 13

My Best Friend

Dear God, I love to look up at the beautiful
blue sky. I know you're up there. I actually
know you're everywhere. Sometimes when
I walk, I can feel you walking with me, and
when I pray, I know you hear me. If I'm very
quiet and still, I hear you talk to me. Thank
you, God, for always being with me and taking
care of me. Thank you for being such a good
friend.

— *Stephen, age 11*

33

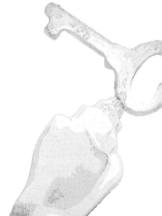

Holding God's Hand

My Lord,
We love you and understand
that you are always
holding our hand.
You help us through good times and bad,
but you are always
holding our hand.
We know we aren't perfect,
but you teach us
the right things to do.
You love us no matter what,
even though we mess up.
God, we love you and understand
that you are always
holding our hand.

— *Katie, age 11*

FAMILY

Prayer for My Mom

Dear Lord,

   Please help my mom get better. She has been
sick for almost three years, and she isn't really
getting better, so can you help us to be strong?
God, help me have a good birthday party with
all my friends and family. Also, I ask you to
help me and my sister get along together and
not give my parents such a hard time. Amen.

— C.J., age 12

35

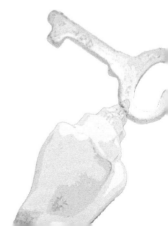

The Gift of My Family

Dear Almighty God,

  Thank you for the gift of my family. Even when we are having problems, we stick together and get through it. Everyone in my family loves each other and wants to be together as much as we can. Sometimes I get sad when my mom has to leave, but my dad is always there to cheer me up. I love you, God, and I will pray to you every day. When I need help I know who to talk to: you and my parents. Amen.

— *Tristan, age 12*

Keep Them Safe

Hello, God, it's me again. I would just like to pray for my two cousins. They are both in the armed forces. Both of them are overseas in dangerous situations. I ask you please to keep them safe and let them return home safely. Amen.

— Kenneth, age 13

37

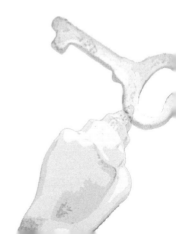

The Love that Comes from My Family

Holy Spirit, families all over the world are experiencing rough times right now. Many families are poor and unhappy. Some parents are even going through divorce. I am so blessed to have my amazing family, and I pray for those who are not as fortunate as I am. Sometimes I see kids upset over things that are happening at home, and it makes me stop and think. Kids all over the world would give anything for the love that comes from my family. I sometimes take having a faith-filled and safe environment at home for granted. Holy Spirit, please guide me to spread the affection coming from my family. Amen.

— *Elizabeth, age 14*

The Blessing of My Brother

Jesus, I would like to thank you for my little brother. He has Down syndrome. After he was born, the doctor told my parents that they can be sure of one thing: there will always be someone in this world who loves them. That's because kids with Down syndrome are so loving. And my brother really is. Thank you for the blessing of my brother, and please help him to keep learning in his classes. Amen.

—Jonathan, age 10

39

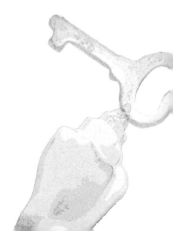

Prayer for My Parents

Dear God,

I would like to take a moment to pray about my parents. They are very important to me, and they always put their children first. They love us and help us with everything we do and need. If we have a problem, they will help us find a solution. If they need something, and I need something, they always help me first. I appreciate everything they do. I love them, and I'm very thankful for them. Amen.

— *Casey, age 12*

EVERYDAY

Thanks for My Family

Dear God,

Thank you for my family. Especially thank you for my older sister for making mistakes so I can learn from them. Also, I would like to thank you for my younger sister. Because of her, I know what it's like to have someone who looks up to me. She always makes me feel special.

I really want to thank you for my younger brother. He is the cutest, funniest Bears fan I have ever seen. He makes me feel loved even though he is only six months old. Thank you for his giggle; it is contagious.

Thank you for my parents, who look after me. Thanks for my mom, who sets the rules to make me a better person. Thanks for my dad, who teaches me about nature and the outdoors. Thank you for my family. Amen.

— Kayla, age 10

41

Thanks for Being There to Listen

Dear God,

Thank you for my family's health and happiness. Although sometimes I take them for granted, I still try to remember to be thankful for them. Thank you also for my best friend. I was pretty scared when I first moved to my new neighborhood, but she made me feel right at home.

Thank you for always being there to listen. Sometimes, when it's hard to express my feelings to my parents, I just close my eyes and think. I believe you're listening. Thank you for all I have. Thank you for the love I feel every day. Thank you for being a friend. Amen.

— Elizabeth, age 10

A New Baby!

Jesus, my mom is expecting a baby.
Sometimes I'm excited that I'm going to have
a little brother. But sometimes I wish things
could just stay the way they are now. Please
help my family to be happy. Take care of my
mom and my baby brother, so everything goes
all right.

Thank you, Jesus.

—Juana, age 10

43

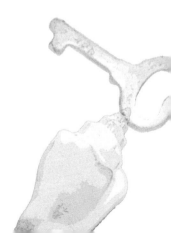

FRIENDS

Such Good Friends

Dear God,
Thank you for all my friends.
My friends are the ones I want to be around.
They're the ones who always have my back.
I like them for who they are,
not for whether they're popular or how they
    look.
My friends always understand
my problems, fears, and concerns.
I will always like them,
no matter what anyone else does or says.
What I mean to say is
that I will always love my friends.
Thank you, God, for loving me and giving me
such good friends. Amen.

— *Megan, age 12*

I'm Having a Rough Time

Dear God,

Please help me do better in school, because I'm having a rough time. These big kids are always picking on my friends and me. Can you please guide bad people to become better people? I will try to be a good friend, too. Amen.

— John, age 11

45

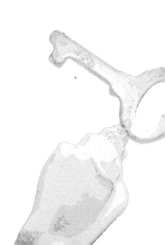

A Prayer for Friendship

Dear Lord,

Friends are so important in this world. Friends have the best times together. Friends can do anything and just laugh. They don't care if they look stupid; they don't care what everyone else thinks. They just do what they do and have a great time doing it. Please, Lord, help my friends and me to remember all this throughout the rest of our lives. Please help me to be there for my friends the way I know they will be there for me.

Even though my friends and I fight, we still love each other like family. Please help my friends and me not to let a fight ruin our friendship. Please watch over my friends and their families. Help them to be healthy and happy. Please, Lord, help me never to lose a friend, whether it's my best friend forever or just a friend I talk to every once in a while. Thank you for friendship. Amen.

— Heather, age 13

My Bully Friend-ish

Dear Lord, I don't really have a best friend
here, because my best friend lives in Israel. I
have this other friend, or so I think, who is
kind of like a bully to me. I tried to separate
us a little, but my life felt empty. Lord, please
help me to figure out how I should handle this.
Amen.

— Emily, age 12

47

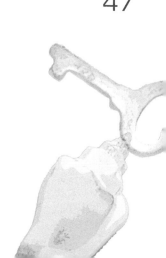

Mixed Messages

Dear Jesus,

I want to talk to you about eating disorders. Some of my friends are always going on diets because they think they're too fat. They say they're not going to get anorexia, but it makes me kind of worried. There are a lot of mixed messages on TV and in magazines. First you see ads everywhere with skinny models, but then you see tons of ads for super-sizing junk food!

Please guide kids to be healthy in their eating, and please help them to talk to their parents if there is a problem. My best friend's older sister goes to a therapist now to get help. My mom says that is a blessing. Thank you, Jesus, for listening.

— *Destiny, age 12*

GIVING THANKS

I Am So Fortunate

God,
I am so fortunate.
I have a great family,
and I have great friends.
I go to Mass on Sundays,
which gives me a chance to be faithful.
I can always count on you.
You always protect me,
which makes me happy.
Thank you!

49

— *Lexi, age 11*

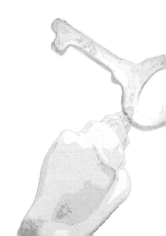

Every Day When I Wake Up

Dear God,

Every day when I wake up, I am thankful to be with my healthy family. Thankful that I have food to eat, clothes to wear, and shelter to protect me from the cold. I don't have to be afraid to go outside, since I live in a peaceful country. I can look out my window and see the natural beauty you have given us. Every day I can laugh, play, and love. I know I am loved by my friends, family, and by you. Thank you, God, for everything. Amen.

— Julia, age 10

50

GRIEF

A Prayer for My Heroes

Dear God,

After a year of worrying, I am glad my uncle is home safely from war. I want to take time on this beautiful day you have given us to say thank you for sending him home safely. The whole year he was over there, I wrote and sent packages to him, but it's just not the same as actually hearing his voice. So once again, God, thank you for answering my prayers.

Sometimes our prayers are not answered the way we would like them to be. So now I pray that a different serviceman, my cousin, is at peace with you in heaven. He died in Afghanistan. Please wrap your arms of comfort and protection around those in the armed forces who continue to protect us. This is my special prayer to you, Almighty God. Amen.

—Jessica, age 10

51

Mr. T.

Dear God,

Ever since Mr. T. died in the summer of 2007, I have been a wreck because I miss giving him hugs every day. He was a good friend and it's hard that he's not here. I would always go to him when I was sad or mad, and he always knew what to say to make me feel better. I trusted him and really cared about him! He will forever be in my heart.

He was the leader of my school, and so many kids and teachers were inspired because of him. He changed my life and so many other people's lives, too. We all miss and love Mr. T.! Please help us to remember him always, Lord. Amen.

— Olivia, age 12

We Miss You, Grandpa

God,

I've been missing someone a lot nowadays. It's my grandpa, Popuse. He was one of the best grandpas ever. Right now my grandma is in a lot of pain, and I wish he could come and comfort her. It's just not the same. When I go to his house, I see my grandma, which is great, but sometimes I wish he was on the couch with her. He was such a great guy, and I really miss him. I'm sure he's in heaven, so can you tell him to watch out for Grandma? Amen.

— Camille, age 10

53

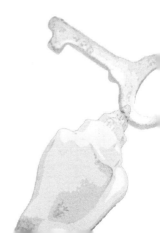

Thank You, Lord, for Heaven

Dear Lord,

When my grandparents and great grandma all died in the same summer, you helped me get through it. I knew they would go to heaven. Also, thank you for helping me remember that when I die, I can go to heaven, too. I can be with all of them in heaven. When you help me to remember this, I can live easier, knowing I don't have to worry about death. Thank you, Lord, for heaven.

— Abby, age 13

A Prayer for My Friend

Dear God,

I would like to say this prayer for one of
my best friends in school. He is almost always
there for me whenever I need him. But he
has a big problem in his family, because his
grandma is sick. I hope she is not suffering
and that she will die a very peaceful death. I
also want my friend to know that I will always
try to be there for him and try to help. I also
thank you for letting him be okay so far, and
when it is over, I hope he will still be okay.
Amen.

— *Edward, age 14*   55

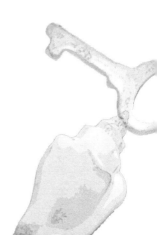

A Great Loss

Lord, if I may ask, please bless those who have a great amount of doubt in their faith. My friend is refusing to go to church because of the great loss of his mother. Lord, may those who have also suffered a great loss recover from their emotional state. Please give him, as well as all those other people in similar situations, the guidance to make the right choices in life. Amen.

— *Ciarra, age 12*

Missing My Grandpa

Dear God,

I just wanted to tell you how happy yet sad I am ever since my grandpa died. I'm happy because he is now happy in heaven with you. I'm sad, though, because now I am left without a grandpa, a grandpa I could actually go and hug. Every Christmas I remember him as if he's still here. Every once in a while, I remember the day he died. I remember that when he was dying, my mom and I had gone out to buy his Christmas gift. My grandpa is my inspiration. I miss him and will also never forget him! Amen.

— Dennise, age 12

57

After a Miscarriage

Dear Jesus,

I'm so sad. My mom was pregnant, but she had a miscarriage. That means my baby sister died before she was born. I love my older brother, but I've been looking forward to having a little sister so much. I had plans for all the fun we would have together!

Why did it happen? I wish she hadn't died. We know she's happy with you, but my family and I are really sad. Please heal our hearts. Amen.

— *Alison, age 11*

Guardian Angels

Because You Love Us

Dear God,

Sometimes we mess up and sometimes we don't even mean to. That's why we have you to help us get through life without doing bad things, and we have you and our guardian angels to keep us safe. Every day we pray to you to keep our families and ourselves safe and for us not to get sick. Thanks for keeping us safe because you love us.

— *Natalie, age 10*

59

My Guardian Angel

My guardian angel,
help me,
show me,
guide me,
teach me,
watch over me in everything I do.
Oh, my dear guardian angel,
show me the way,
be there for me when I get lonely,
sad,
angry,
or jealous.
Guide me to heaven. Amen.

— *Sarah, age 11*

Hopes and Dreams

Together, Our World

Jesus, a prayer is a symbol of our hopes, fears,
   and dreams.
A prayer tells you who we are and who we
   aspire to become.
Every day we face challenges that test whether
   or not each of us is your disciple.
And what I ask for is that you extend your
gracious, forgiving hand to me and help me
reach for the stars and have a glimpse of what
   I could be.
Just a small glance of what I could do to
   change this world.
Filled with your love and peace, I pray that I
will always be willing to lend a helping hand
   to those who need it.
Please give the world the gift of cooperation
and wisdom so that we can change it to be
   what you originally intended,
a place where everybody can share in the peace
and love you have given us.
Together, our world.

— *Maria, age 13*

ILLNESS

Prayer for Nurses

God, please protect the nurses who care for children. Help them to be patient, kind, and caring. Keep their minds sharp and prepared to help those in need, especially in emergencies. Keep them safe from illness and disease as they care for others. Help them to help me get better. Please help us to care for others as they care for us. Amen.

— Christopher, age 10

Oh, My Heavenly Father

Dear God,

I would like to pray for my grandma. She is very ill with cancer. I want to pray for her because she is special to me. We share the same name and personality. I would love for her to feel better and get out of the hospital. She is eighty-three years old, and I hope it is your will that she will recover. God, bless her and watch over my family. Amen.

— *Rachel, age 11*

63

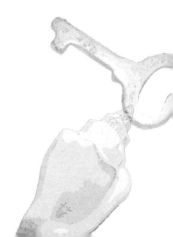

Please Help

Dear God,

Hi, God, how are you? Please help my uncle, who is really sick. If it is your will that he join you in heaven, please welcome him warmly. I was also wondering if you could help me figure out a way to resolve something with a friend who won't listen to my apologies. Please forgive me for everything I have done wrong. I'm still trying to do my best at being respectful. Best wishes,

— *Anna, age 11*

Hi, It's Me, Taylor

Dear God,

Hi, it's me, Taylor. I want to thank you for everything I have. I'm very lucky to have such a special family and friends. I need to ask you to watch over my grandpa. He's in the hospital and is very sick. Please give him all the strength he needs to get better. His heart is very weak. I miss him and can't wait for him to be healthy again. Amen.

— *Taylor, age 10*

65

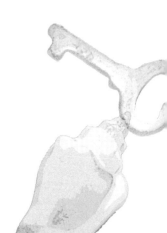

MEDIA AWARENESS

Media Choices

Dear Jesus,

I like seeing movies with my friends, listening to music, and spending time on the computer. But a lot of television, music, video games, etc., are pretty violent and have disrespectful language. My parents have rules at home, but sometimes I have to use my own judgment, like when I'm out with friends or at their houses. Jesus, please guide me to make good choices about the media I use. Amen.

— *Dennis, age 12*

MONEY

Grateful for What I Have

Dear God,

I was really counting on going to camp
this summer. But my family couldn't afford it.
It seems like my parents are always worried
about money and making ends meet. It stresses
them out, and it's kind of hard for me, too.
I know I should be grateful for what I have,
but sometimes it doesn't seem like enough.
I promise I'll try harder, and please bless my
parents, who work so hard. Also please bless
kids who don't have enough to eat or a place
to live. Amen.

67

— *Sheila, age 11*

Spending Money

Dear Jesus,

I just got a regular babysitting job, and I finally have my own spending money! My mom wants me to put some in my savings account and donate some to charity, but the rest I can use however I want. I don't want to waste it, though. Please help me to be responsible with my money and still have fun! Thanks, Jesus. Amen.

— Marsha, age 13

PROBLEMS IN OUR WORLD

Peace Prayer

Dear God,

When I listen to the news with my mom, we hear about so many violent things happening around the world—wars, terrorist attacks, people being killed for reasons that don't even make sense. God, please protect the people who have to live every day being scared of losing people they love, or even their own lives. And please help the leaders in every country make smart decisions that will make the violence stop, so there can be peace in the world. Amen.

— *Tasha, age 12*

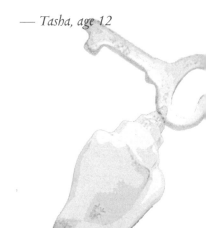

A Better Life

I pray for a better life for those in need
    and for a better environment.
I pray that together the world can end violence
    and cruelty.
I ask you, Lord, to help my friends and family
    in times of sickness.
I pray for anyone who abuses people or
    animals,
that they may come to understand right from
    wrong.
I pray for all who have been abused, people or
    animals.
I pray for families who have lost someone close
    to them.
I pray for cures for diseases.
I hope I can help make the world a better
place, and I ask you, Lord,
to be there along the way.
Thank you for blessing me with this life and
with everything I have. Amen.

— *Amanda, age 12*

My Prayer for Justice

The world is like a deck of cards.
There are kings and there are sixes.
There are reds and there are blacks.
But with one missing, the deck is incomplete.
So, God, guide humanity in our fight against
    racism.
Only you can change hearts.
Black, whites, Latinos, Asians, who cares?
We are the human race.
Religion, money, race, or even the clothes we
wear should not label us.
Justice, spirit, and our love should.
It shouldn't matter whether you're from Iran or
    Mexico.
The things that really matter are love for
family, trust, and mutual respect.
God, I love you. Amen.

— *Carlos, age 13*

Prayer for the Young at War

Dear God,

I would like to pray for all the soldiers who are fighting in wars. They have to leave home and their families, and some of them are only eighteen years old! I pray that they are safe and that they all return to their homes as soon as possible. Please watch over them all and keep them protected. Amen.

— *Kristin, age 13*

Lord, Help Those Who Can't Stop

Dear Lord,
Please help people to overcome addictions.
Help those who are addicted to drugs.
Help those who can't stop smoking cigarettes.
Help those who can't stop drinking.
Help my uncle, who is in recovery.
Help all the families of people who are
addicted, because it's really hard for them, too.
Lord, hear my prayer. Amen.

— *Luis, age 12*

73

Why Do People Fight?

Dear God,

Why do people fight? Do they just not like each other? Why couldn't they just talk about it? Sometimes I think about how the people who are living in the middle of wars must feel. I would feel awful if I were them. Please help all those who are trapped in war. Amen.

— *Maggie, age 11*

74

A Prayer for Safety in Families

Dear God,

Please keep everyone in families safe from domestic violence. People who love each other shouldn't hurt each other. It is never okay. I pray to you to keep everyone in every family safe from violence. Amen.

— *Amanda, age 11*

Please Help Our Community

Dear Jesus,

I just heard about a teacher at my brother's high school who got shot. It seems like there is so much violence in our community. Sometimes it's gang members, and sometimes it's just random. Either way, I'm afraid that something bad could happen to me or to someone I care about. God, I know you love us always. Please help everyone in our community to remember that no one needs to hurt people to feel safe or powerful. Amen.

— *Rasheed, age 11*

SCHOOL

The First Day of School

Dear Lord,
Tomorrow is the first day of school.
I am really, really scared.
Lord, please give me the courage and guidance
I need. Amen.

— Ailish, age 11

77

Prayer for My School and Friends

Jesus,

    My school is an important place. It was there I learned to read, write, and to praise and love God. When I was very little, I didn't know anything about God or the Church. When I first came here, I thought I would stick out. I thought that people at school would judge me just because my eyes, my culture, and my name were all different. But a couple of days later, I met some great people who are now my friends. God, please keep my friends safe. Amen.

— Resseka, age 10

I Do Try

Lord, please make my days in school go easier. Reading is a little harder for me than for most of the kids in my class, and no one, not even the teachers, seems to understand. I do try, but it doesn't seem to be enough. I ask for your blessing and your help. Amen.

— *Matthew, age 11*

79

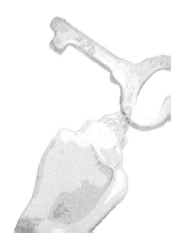

EVERYDAY

In Fifth Grade

Dear Lord,

In fifth grade, there's a lot going on. There's so much homework. Please guide me to make the right choices and help me to work hard. Please help me to choose the right friends. Amen.

— Kirsten, age 10

Teachers

Thank you, God, for the many teachers
you have given me and who have led me
through my life. Without them, I don't know
where I would be. My teachers have led me
academically, mentally, and religiously. Thank
for you these wonderful gifts. Amen.

— *Kristen, age 12*

81

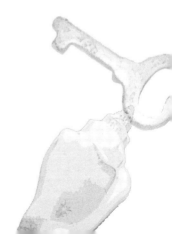

Give Me the Grace

Abba,

My love, my Father. I need to tell you how I feel about the way school is going. I'm feeling a lot of stress. With all the assignments due, it seems as if I have no time of my own. I wish and hope that I can stay strong and be confident. Help me and please give me the grace, my dear Father.

— Dani, age 11

A Prayer for Help

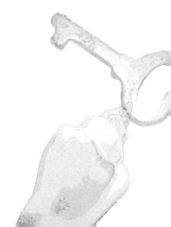

Dear God,

I need help getting better grades. I know you can't do it for me, but you can give me the hope and courage I need. I need help trying to be with people, not just being by myself. I need help participating in school. God, please give me strength and spirit. Amen.

— *Carissa, age 11*

83

Graduation

Dear God,
This year is the year
we graduate.
The year we go our separate ways.
We might never see each other again.
That's a scary thought!
Not seeing the kids you grew up with.
The ones you share memories with.
The ones who know you
like no one else
will ever know you.
The ones who can relate to you no matter
   what.
God, bless us and give us courage
as we move forward. Amen.

— Jordan, age 13

Sports

Lucky

Dear Jesus,
Help me to remember today
It's not whether I win or lose,
It's how I play.

To conduct myself just like you,
With respect for the game, other players,
And the coaches, too.

I'm very lucky to be here,
To be part of this team,
To hear the crowd cheer.

Thank you, Jesus, for the opportunity to
  compete.
I'll try to be gracious and dignified,
And to remember I'm a lucky athlete. Amen.

— Allie, age 12

Skate with Us, God

Dear God, please bless my hockey team. I ask that you skate along with us and that no one gets hurt. I ask that you help all of us to remember that the most important thing is to do our best. I ask that you be at our sides and with our families, too. I also ask that everyone has fun and no one gets mad and no one yells at the referees. Amen.

— Rory, age 10

86

STRESS

Pressure Points

Dear God,

Lately I've been under a lot of pressure, and not just "peer pressure." It's just that everything has been adding up: school, family, and friends. Not that my friends are a problem; they're great, it's just that they're under the same pressure. Being eighth graders, we have a lot of schoolwork, and having it all due at the same time is very frustrating. So I am praying that you give us the hope and strength we need to get through the year. Thank you!

87

— *Christina, age 13*

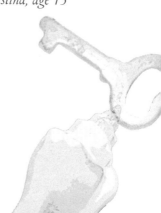

A Prayer for Sleep

O dear God, please help all the people like me who can't get enough sleep because they are up late doing sports, activities, studying, homework, or other things. God, please help us. Amen.

— Samantha, age 11

A Really Bad Day

Dear Jesus,

I've had a really bad day. I'm not blaming you. I know you are kind enough to give me a house and a family, and some kids don't have all that. I'm not complaining. I'm just saying, could you please help me out next time things get hard, and can you help out the kids who have it harder than I do? Amen.

— *Madie, age 10*

89

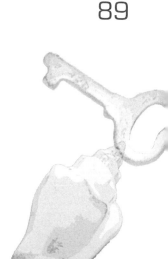

A Hard Time

Lord Jesus, help me to be more responsible. I'm having a really hard time taking care of all my studying. I want to be like my parents, the way they manage to take care of my brother and me. I'm full of thanks for helping me pass most of my tests. I prayed to you, O Lord, before the tests. The tests I didn't get good grades on, I didn't study for a lot, though. Thank you for teaching me a lesson. I will try to be more responsible and listen to my parents. In Jesus' name, amen.

— *Dylan, age 11*

90

Trying My Best

O God, Help Me

O God, help me not to feel defeat when I get
   bad grades.
O God, help me to get over my failures and try
   harder next time.
O God, hear this prayer and help me realize
   that it's okay as long as I try. Amen.

— *Amanda, age 11*

91

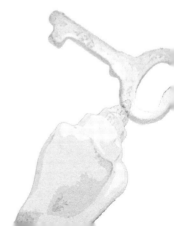

Thanks for Listening

God, please help me in my everyday life. Though I study hard, I still pray to you, hoping I will do well in school. I ask you to help me because I'm under a lot of pressure. Between having a lot of homework and being involved in a lot of activities, I hope I can get through this tough part of life. I'll try my best, and with your help I may be able to reach my goals in life. Thanks for listening. Amen.

— *Patricia, age 13*

To Do My Best

Dear God,
Help me to work hard in school and to get my
    homework done each night.
Help me to do my best on tests, too.
Help me to be a good friend to my peers, my
    parents, and my pets.
Help me to be successful as I work to become
    an Eagle Scout.
Help me to master my Tae Kwon Do skills and
    reach my goal to be a black belt.
Help me to do my best at whatever I try.
Amen.

— Charles, age 11

I Should At Least Try

Dear God,

I usually try to do my best on everything. But sometimes I get bored, tired, or just don't want to do whatever it is. Even though I can't do everything, I should at least try. Amen.

— Mary, age 11

I Will Try

Jesus,
Sometimes
we want things
that aren't important,
but all we do is ask for
more, when we should be
appreciating what we have—
the important things like food, drink,
shelter, family, health, and you! We know
in our hearts that we shouldn't wake up mad,
saying, "Man, I have to go to school";
instead, it should be, "I wonder what
I'll do today!" I know that I don't
always wake up with
a smile, but I will
try.
Amen.

— Maddie, age 10

PART TWO

PRAYERS TO FAVORITE SAINTS

Introduction

In intercessory prayer, we can ask for
God's blessing for others, living or dead.
We can also ask Mary and the saints, God's
friends in heaven, to intercede—to pray
with us—either for ourselves or on behalf
of others.

In this section, you'll find prayers from
kids who are asking favorite saints to pray
with them and for them for many different
reasons. Do you have a favorite saint? How
would you ask that saint to intercede for
you or for someone who's special to you?

Saint Adelaide (931–999)

Saint Adelaide was a princess from Burgundy. She married a king, but three years later he was poisoned by his enemies. Her second husband was King Otto of Germany. After twenty-two happy years of marriage, King Otto died. Adelaide's oldest son's wife turned against Adelaide, forcing her to leave the palace. Eventually her son begged her forgiveness, and Adelaide returned. She worked to help the poor and built many monasteries and convents. Saint Adelaide is the patron saint of widows, second marriages, and stepfamilies.

Dear Saint Adelaide,

I put myself in your hands, and I ask that you help me to be a good stepdaughter and daughter. I ask that you help me find understanding, patience, and love to deal with my stepparents and parents. Please help me to forgive my parents and stepparents when they get mad at me, and help them to forgive me when I get mad at them. I also ask that you help my parents and stepparents to understand and love me, because I am a child of God. Amen.

— *Logan, age 10*

Saint Angela Merici (1470–1540)

Born in Italy, Angela joined the Secular Franciscan Order when she was thirteen, beginning a life of prayer. Later Angela and several friends started a school to teach girls from poor families. During a pilgrimage to the Holy Land, Angela suddenly lost her sight, but praying before a crucifix, she miraculously regained it. She began what would become the Institute of Saint Ursula (the Ursuline Sisters), the Church's first congregation of teaching sisters. She is the patron saint of disabled and physically challenged people.

Dear Saint Angela,

For all those who are suffering from illness and disease, pray for us.

For all those who are handicapped or disabled, pray for us.

For all those who have lost a loved one, pray for us.

For all those who have troubles and worries, pray for us.

For all those who need our help and support, pray for us.

Thank you, Saint Angela, for helping us every day. Amen.

— *Gabriela, age 12*

Saint Anthony of Padua (1195–1231)

Anthony was an Augustinian friar in Portugal. At the age of twenty-five, he transferred to the Friars Minor, a new order begun by Francis of Assisi. He went to Africa as a missionary, but on the return trip, a storm forced his ship to land in Italy. There Anthony quietly performed humble tasks in a friary. One day he was asked to preach to a crowd of important people, who were very impressed. For the rest of his life, Anthony traveled and preached God's Word. Saint Anthony is the patron saint of finding lost articles and of the poor.

Dear Saint Anthony,

People say, "When you need to find anything, pray to Saint Anthony."

Well, I'm praying to you. I need to find myself. I'm going through those years when I'll need to find the person I am going to be for the rest of my life. Help and guide me through the times coming up when I will need you the most. Thank you for being here.

Love,

— *Megan, age 13*

Saint Cecilia (second century)

Cecilia was a Roman noblewoman who is said to have been "singing in her heart a hymn of love for Jesus." Married at a young age, she convinced her husband and his brother to convert to Christianity. Both were arrested and martyred for their beliefs. After their deaths, Cecilia was arrested, too. Her captors demanded that she make a sacrifice to false gods. She refused and was killed as well. Saint Cecilia is the patron saint of musicians, singers, and poets.

O Saint Cecilia,
please help me with my music.
Let it be soothing
to all who hear it. Amen.

— *Mai Linh, age 11*

Saint Bakhita (1868–1947)

Bakhita was born in Africa in Darfur, Sudan. Kidnapped by slave traders at the age of nine, she was repeatedly sold to harsh owners. When she was a teenager, a family took her to Italy. There she attended the school of the Canossian Sisters. When the family returned to Africa, Bakhita refused to leave Italy, where slavery was illegal. She joined the Canossian congregation and became a religious sister. She forgave all who had treated her unkindly, always caring lovingly for others. Saint Bakhita is the patron saint of workers.

Saint Bakhita, even when you were enslaved, you never gave up and never complained. Please help me not to complain, and please pray for people who are less fortunate than I am. Please pray for those who are ill, those who are serving in the military, and people caught in war, natural disasters, and terrorist attacks.

I would ask you to pray for my family, my stepfamily in the Philippines, my friends, and all my teachers. Please help me always to stay faithful to God and to be honest. Help me to be kinder to others and not to whine for things I don't really need. I pray for peace on earth. Amen.

— *Erin, age 10*

103

Saint Clare of Assisi (1193–1253)

Clare was the daughter of a wealthy family in Italy. At the age of eighteen, inspired by the preaching of Francis of Assisi, she ran away from home to give her life to God. With Francis, she founded the women's religious order now known as the Poor Clares. Dedicated to imitating Jesus in a life of poverty and prayer, Clare served as abbess of her convent for over forty years. Because she is believed to have had miraculous visions of events occurring far away, Saint Clare is the patron saint of television!

Dear Saint Clare,

There are many things I wish God would
    change in the world,

but there is one thing I especially would like to
    be changed.

I would like to change the fact that so many
people are suffering from diseases.

That includes my older sister, who has
    diabetes.

Her life is more complicated than some, which
    doesn't seem fair.

You are my patron saint, so I would like to ask
you, Saint Clare, to be sure that God hears my
prayer. Amen.

— *Claire, age 12*

Saint Elizabeth of Hungary
(1207–1231)

Elizabeth's father was a king. Elizabeth married Ludwig, the ruler of Thuringia. Six years later, Ludwig died; his royal relatives forced the princess and her children to leave the castle. Soon they were taken in by Elizabeth's family, but she never forgot the fear and hunger of being homeless. She spent the rest of her life as a Third Order Franciscan, establishing a hospital to serve the poor of her city. Saint Elizabeth is the patron of hospitals, shelters, and meal centers.

Dear Saint Elizabeth,

You did so many things to help people. Now you are still with us, giving us a great role model. You showed us that kindness counts. Being a princess, you had quite a bit of power. But you weren't unfair—you brought food to the poor and cared for sick people.

There are many sick people in the world today. Please be with them, Saint Elizabeth— help them to get well, or if it's God's will, welcome them into heaven. Please help everyone to find peace among war, comfort among sadness, sharing among greed, and health among sickness.

With love and thanks,

— Peyton, age 10

Saint Francis of Assisi (1181–1226)

As a young man in Assisi, Italy, Francis was fond of fine clothes, money, and fun. His dream was to be a knight, and he went to war when he was twenty. After being captured and imprisoned, Francis heard God's voice telling him, "Rebuild my church." Francis gave up his wealth and started helping the poor. He became Christ's knight, preaching tirelessly and living, like Jesus, in poverty and love. Eventually others joined him, and he became the founder of the great Franciscan Order. Saint Francis is the patron saint of animals and of the environment.

Dear Saint Francis,

   You protect and love animals, as we all should. You love them with all your heart. You love every dog and cat, every carnivore and herbivore, every dolphin and shark, and every animal big and small. You care about not only us, but also for every part of nature on the planet earth. Please help us to stop poverty, disasters, and global warming. And please help us to save the rain forests. You give us the courage you had and much love, and we thank you. Amen.

— *Nicole (age 12)*

Saint Geneviève (422–512)

Geneviève grew up near Paris, France. She became a nun at a young age, and God began to send her visions soon after. War broke out, and soon word came that the city was about to be invaded. In their fear, the citizens wanted to flee, but Geneviève had a holy vision. She convinced them all to pray with her for the city's safety. The invading army stopped and turned around! Saint Geneviève is honored as the patron saint of the city of Paris.

Dear Saint Geneviève,

Hello! My name is Jennifer, just like yours, only in English. I'm praying to you because I admire you for being a saint and helping people. If you can do it, so can I. You're a great inspiration. When I have problems, I look to you for help and for comfort. Because you are my patron saint, I know you'll help me. I love the fact that you devoted your life to God and to helping people. That's amazing. Thanks for listening to my prayer, and you will be in my heart forever.

Peacefully yours,

— *Jennifer, age 13*

Saint Gerard (1725–1755)

Gerard Majella was born in Muro, Italy. After training as a tailor, he became a Redemptorist lay brother, serving his community at various times as a gardener, hospital aide, doorman, and tailor. He was a hard worker and a model of obedience. Brother Gerard was said to possess the gift of bilocation (being in two places at the same time) and to have powers to cure the sick. Saint Gerard is the patron saint of expectant mothers, childbirth, and unborn children.

Holy Saint Gerard, please bless and help those
   who are expecting babies.
I pray to you and to all the other saints for
children who are abandoned and lost, and
I pray for all children who have no homes.
Amen.

— *Ciarán, age 10*

Saint Ignatius of Loyola (1491–1556)

This famous saint was born into a noble Spanish family. He entered the army and won honors for his bravery in battle. Wounded by a cannonball and confined to bed, he began reading about Jesus and the saints. After his recovery, he began studying for the priesthood. He and six other men founded a religious order called the Society of Jesus, known as the Jesuits. Their followers became missionaries, teaching and preaching all over the world. Saint Ignatius is the patron saint of religious retreats and of soldiers.

Dear Saint Ignatius,
Please help the soldiers in war.
Help them return safely to their homes.
Help them to recover from their injuries, the way you did when the cannonball hit your leg.
Please help us to end war and to work for peace. Amen.

— John, age 11

109

Saint Joan of Arc (1412–1431)

Joan grew up in a small French village. As a teenager, she repeatedly heard the voices of saints urging her to save her country in war. Soon she led an army into the city of Orleans, winning a great victory for France. After many more battles, she was captured and charged with witchcraft and heresy (denying the truth of the Catholic faith). Although the charge was later declared untrue, she was burned at the stake, dying with her faith in Jesus intact. Saint Joan is the patron saint of France, servicewomen, and soldiers.

Saint Joan of Arc, I pray to you for courage. Help me to be brave when I am scared. Give me confidence to overcome my fears. Give me strength to avoid temptation. I want to follow your example of bravery and obedience to God. Amen.

— *Rachel, age 10*

Saint Joseph (first century)

Joseph was a Jewish man who was descended from King David. Originally from Bethlehem, he became a carpenter in Nazareth and was married to Mary, the Mother of Jesus. As Mary's loving husband, it was his privilege and joy to help raise and care for God's own Son. Humble, gentle, and wise, Joseph is revered today as a model father and husband. Saint Joseph is the patron of the Universal Church as well as of carpenters, families, and the dying.

Dear Saint Joseph,

I'm going to make my Confirmation pretty soon, and I'm going to choose Joseph as my Confirmation name. My grandfather's name was Joseph, too, but he died when I was just a little kid. So taking Joseph for my Confirmation name is a way for me to honor him as well as you. It was really great the way you took care of Mary and of Jesus. Thank you for being our caretaker, Saint Joseph, and for being such a good role model. Amen.

— *Adalius, age 13*

Saint Jude (first century)

Jude was one of Jesus' original twelve apostles. He was sometimes called Thaddeus, which means "brave one." After Jesus' ascension into heaven, Jude, with the rest of the apostles and Mary, received the Holy Spirit on the first Pentecost. Afterward he went to Persia to evangelize with Saint Simon, and the two were martyred there. Saint Jude is known as the patron saint of hospitals and of causes that seem hopeless.

Saint Jude,

I am praying to you because you know what it feels like when nothing is going right. More than anything else, I want to make the baseball team this year, but it's going to be tough. A lot of really great players are trying out. I know I'm not as good as some of them.

Even though God knows what's best for us, I hope you can help me figure out a way to work hard and make the team. Thank you for everything. Amen.

— *Dan, age 13*

Saint Julie Billiart (1751–1816)

As a young woman in France, Julie always found time to pray, visit the sick, and teach religion classes. One day she became very ill and was paralyzed. Although she was confined to bed, more and more young women began coming to her for spiritual advice. With Mother Julie as their leader, they started the religious congregation of the Sisters of Notre Dame de Namur. After being paralyzed for twenty-two years, Julie was cured after making a special novena (nine days of prayer). Saint Julie is a patron saint for people suffering from poverty and from sickness.

Dear Saint Julie,

Help us to smile throughout the day and to be pleasant to whomever we meet. Help us feel the presence of God at every corner we cross. Let light shine upon us as you guide us into heaven. Amen.

— *Julia, age 10*

113

Mary, the Mother of God
(first century)

Mary, the daughter of Joachim and Anne, lived in Nazareth in Judea. God sent the angel Gabriel to ask Mary to be the mother of his Son. When Mary answered yes, she conceived Jesus through the power of the Holy Spirit. Mary married Joseph, and together they loved and raised Jesus. After Jesus' crucifixion, resurrection, and ascension, Mary and the apostles received the Holy Spirit at the first Pentecost. Mary, the Blessed Mother, is the mother of us all. She reigns forever as Queen of Heaven.

Dear Mother Mary,

Please help me to be just like you. When you were young, you listened to your mother, Saint Anne. When the angel came to tell you that you were to be the mother of Jesus, you said "yes" to God. When your Son, our Savior, Jesus Christ, suffered his passion, you never left his side. Please help me to love and trust God always, as you did. You are the Blessed Mother of us all. Help me and everyone else to love and cherish God always. Amen.

— *Lily, age 10*

Saint Paul (first century)

Paul, born in Tarsus as Saul, opposed the new religion that became known as Christianity. In fact, he received permission to hunt down and arrest Christians. On the road to Damascus, Saul saw a bright light and heard the voice of God. Temporarily blinded and then cured, he became known as Paul and was himself converted to Christianity. Paul traveled and wrote extensively, bringing the Good News of Christ to countless people all over the known world. He was finally martyred for his faith. Saint Paul is the patron saint of journalists and authors.

Saint Paul, you were a great man. You weren't afraid of being put to death because of your beliefs. You worked harder than most saints. You were the best saint ever, in my opinion.

— *Jeremy, age 12*

Saint Pio of Pietrelcina (1887–1968)

As a teenager in Italy, Francisco Forgione entered the Capuchin Friary and took the religious name Brother Pio. Later ordained a priest, Padre (Father) Pio received the special grace of stigmata (wounds like Jesus' in the hands, feet, and side). Padre Pio's other gifts from God included heavenly visions, prophecy, bilocation, and levitation (being raised above the ground with no support). He was renowned as a confessor and spiritual director. Saint Pio is the patron saint of adolescents and of civil defense volunteers.

Saint Pio, thank you for showing us that even when we suffer, we should always love God. God showed us that he is all-powerful by doing miracles through you. When someone is sick, I will pray to you because I know you will help. You are a very inspiring saint! Amen.

— *Sarah, age 11*

Saint Rose of Lima (1586–1617)

This Peruvian saint was born as Isabel. Because of her beauty, her family called her Rose. Rose, a very spiritual young woman, understood that inward beauty and virtue are more important than outward appearances. She dedicated her life to God, joining the Dominican Third Order, a religious order for laypersons. Living in a small hut on her parents' property, Rose worked hard at gardening, sewing, and helping the poor. She is the patron saint of the Americas, the Philippines, and the West Indies.

Dear Saint Rose,

Please help me to always be as reverent as you. I want to help people as you did, doing works of charity. I admire you for the fact that you made so many sacrifices out of devotion and love of God. Can you help me to focus on my studies and be good in school?

Thank you for watching me and keeping me safe. Saint Rose, please continue to guide me and help me make good choices. Amen.

— Nina, age 12

117

Blessed Teresa of Calcutta
(1910–1997)

Agnes Gonxha Bojaxhiu was born in Macedonia and joined the Loreto Sisters when she was eighteen. Sent to India to teach in missionary schools, Teresa heard a call from God to leave the Loreto congregation to live with and serve the "poorest of the poor." Mother Teresa founded the Missionaries of Charity, working tirelessly to feed, educate, and provide care for thousands living in poverty in India and around the globe. Many pray to Blessed Teresa to intercede on behalf of leper patients, the poor, and for the welfare of India.

Blessed Teresa, please pray for the poor in need of food and shelter, that they may be able to provide for their families and find a place where they can be safe.

Please ask almighty God to guide us, the children of the world, to realize what others are going through so that we may have to compassion to help them. Amen.

— *Stephanie, age 13*

Saint Thérèse of Lisieux
(1873–1897)

Thérèse, often called "The Little Flower," lived in France. When she was fifteen, she entered the Carmelite Order. Thérèse had a strong desire to become a saint. She asked God's help in doing every small duty in the best way possible: prayerfully, humbly, and with love. This "little way" of holiness became known around the world when her autobiography, The Story of a Soul, *was published. She died of tuberculosis at the age of twenty-four. Saint Thérèse is the patron saint of missionaries, tuberculosis patients, and florists.*

Saint Thérèse, please help me to be a little
    flower like you today.
Help me to stop and think before I say or do
    anything I shouldn't.
Ask God to bless even those I don't really like.
Please help me to be patient with everyone I
    encounter today.
Thank you, Saint Thérèse.

—Julie, age 11

119

PART THREE

TRADITIONAL CATHOLIC PRAYERS

TRADITIONAL

Introduction

When it's hard to find the words to pray, we can turn to many beloved traditional prayers. These prayers have been handed down through generations of believers. Praying them helps us stay connected to our Catholic faith, to each other, and to God.

The Sign of the Cross

In the name of the Father,
and of the Son,
and of the Holy Spirit. Amen.

Our Father

Our Father, who art in heaven,
hallowed be thy name.
Thy kingdom come,
thy will be done on earth
as it is in heaven.
Give us this day
our daily bread,
and forgive us our trespasses,
as we forgive those
who trespass against us.
And lead us not into temptation,
but deliver us from evil. Amen.

123

Hail Mary

Hail Mary, full of grace,
the Lord is with you.
Blessed are you among women,
and blessed is the fruit of your womb, Jesus.
Holy Mary, Mother of God,
pray for us sinners
now and at the hour of our death.
Amen.

Glory

Glory
to the Father,
and to the Son,
and to the Holy Spirit:
as it was in the beginning, is now,
and will be for ever. Amen.

Apostles' Creed

I believe in God, the Father almighty,
　creator of heaven and earth.

I believe in Jesus Christ, his only Son, our Lord.
　He was conceived by the power of the Holy
　　Spirit and born of the Virgin Mary.
　He suffered under Pontius Pilate,
　　was crucified, died, and was buried.
　He descended to the dead.
　On the third day he rose again.
　He ascended into heaven,
　　and is seated at the right hand of the
　　Father.
　He will come again to judge the living and
　　the dead.

I believe in the Holy Spirit,
　the holy catholic Church,
　the communion of saints,
　the forgiveness of sins,
　the resurrection of the body,
　and the life everlasting. Amen.

Act of Contrition

My God,
I am sorry for my sins with all my heart.
In choosing to do wrong
and failing to do good,
I have sinned against you
whom I should love above all things.
I firmly intend, with your help,
to do penance,
to sin no more,
and to avoid whatever leads me to sin.

Our Savior Jesus Christ
suffered and died for us.
In his name, my God, have mercy.

Prayer for the Dead

Eternal rest grant to them, O Lord,
and let perpetual light shine upon them.

Angel of God

Angel of God,
my guardian dear,
to whom God's love
entrusts me here.
Ever this day
be at my side,
to light and guard,
to rule and guide.
Amen.

127

The Jesus Prayer

Lord Jesus, Son of God,
have mercy on me.

Prayer before Meals

Bless us, O Lord,
and these your gifts
which we are about to receive from your
  bounty,
through Christ our Lord. Amen.

Prayer after Meals

We give you thanks
for all your benefits,
O loving God,
you who live and reign
for ever. Amen.

Act of Faith

O my God,
I firmly believe that you are one God
in three Divine Persons,
Father, Son, and Holy Spirit;
I believe that your Divine Son became man
and died for our sins,
and that he will come again
to judge the living and the dead.
I believe these
and all the truths
which the holy Catholic Church teaches,
because you have revealed them
who can neither deceive nor be deceived.

129

Act of Hope

O my God,
relying on your infinite goodness and promises,
I hope to obtain pardon of my sins,
the help of your grace,
and life everlasting,
through the merits of Jesus Christ,
my Lord and Redeemer.

Act of Love

O my God,
I love you above all things,
with my whole heart and soul,
because you are all good and worthy of all
   love.
I love my neighbor as myself for the love of
   you.
I forgive all who have injured me
and ask pardon of all whom I have injured.

131

Morning Offering

O Jesus,
through the Immaculate Heart of Mary,
I offer you my prayers, works,
joys, and sufferings
of this day, for all the intentions
of your Sacred Heart,
in union with the Holy Sacrifice of the Mass
throughout the world,
in reparation for my sins,
for the intentions of all my relatives and
    friends,
and in particular
for the intentions of the Holy Father.
Amen.

The Rosary

The Rosary is a prayer that helps Catholics to remember the lives of Jesus and Mary. While we think about them, we pray the Our Father, the Hail Mary, and the Glory. We pray using a chain of beads called rosary beads. The mysteries of the Rosary consist of many different events from the lives of Jesus and Mary. There are four different sets of mysteries: the joyful mysteries, the mysteries of light, the sorrowful mysteries, and the glorious mysteries. We think about one set of mysteries every time we pray the Rosary.

The Joyful Mysteries

1. The Annunciation—Mary becomes the Mother of God.
2. The Visitation—Mary visits St. Elizabeth.
3. The Nativity—Jesus is born in a stable in Bethlehem.
4. The Presentation of Jesus in the Temple—Mary and Joseph present Jesus to God.
5. The Finding of Jesus in the Temple—Mary and Joseph find Jesus talking about God his Father.

The Mysteries of Light

1. The Baptism of Jesus—John baptizes Jesus.
2. The Wedding at Cana—Jesus works his first miracle.

3. Jesus Announces God's Kingdom—Jesus teaches the people to turn their hearts to God.

4. The Transfiguration—Jesus shines with the glory of God.

5. Jesus Gives Us the Holy Eucharist—Jesus offers us his Body and Blood as food to make us strong in love and holiness.

The Sorrowful Mysteries

1. The Agony in the Garden—Jesus suffers and prays.

2. The Scourging at the Pillar—Jesus is tied up and whipped.

3. The Crowning with Thorns—the soldiers make fun of Jesus.

4. The Carrying of the Cross—Jesus carries his heavy cross.

5. The Crucifixion—Jesus is nailed to the cross and dies for us.

The Glorious Mysteries

1. The Resurrection—Jesus rises from the dead.

2. The Ascension—Jesus goes back to heaven.

3. The Descent of the Holy Spirit—the Holy Spirit comes down upon Mary and the apostles.

4. The Assumption—Mary is taken body and soul to heaven.
5. The Coronation—Mary is crowned queen of heaven and earth.

How We Pray the Rosary

1. Make the Sign of the Cross and pray the Apostles' Creed.
2. Pray the Our Father.
3. Pray three Hail Marys.

4. Pray the Glory, name the first mystery, and pray the Our Father.
5. Pray ten Hail Marys.
6. Pray the Glory, name the second mystery, and pray the Our Father.
7. Repeat steps 5 and 6 until you reach the end.
8. Pray the Glory and the Hail, Holy Queen. Kiss the crucifix.

135

Hail, Holy Queen

Hail, holy Queen, Mother of Mercy,
our life, our sweetness, and our hope.
To you do we cry, poor banished children of
    Eve;
to you do we send up our sighs,
mourning and weeping in this valley of tears.
Turn then, most gracious advocate,
your eyes of mercy toward us,
and after this our exile,
show unto us the blessed fruit of your womb,
    Jesus.
O clement, O loving, O sweet Virgin Mary.

Memorare

Remember, O most gracious Virgin Mary,
that never was it known
that anyone who fled to your protection,
implored your help,
or sought your intercession was left unaided.
Inspired by this confidence,
I fly unto you,
O Virgin of virgins, my mother;
to you do I come,
before you I stand, sinful and sorrowful.
O Mother of the Word Incarnate,
despise not my petitions,
but in your mercy hear and answer me.
Amen.

137

The Angelus

The Angelus, which honors the moment when Mary said "yes" to becoming the mother of Jesus, is traditionally prayed three times a day: in the morning, at noon, and at night.

V. The angel spoke God's message to Mary,
R. and she conceived of the Holy Spirit.

Hail, Mary.

V. "I am the lowly servant of the Lord:
R. let it be done to me according to your word."

Hail, Mary.

V. And the Word became flesh
R. and lived among us.

Hail, Mary.

V. Pray for us, holy Mother of God,
R. that we may become worthy of the promises of Christ.

Let us pray.

Lord,
fill our hearts with your grace:
once, through the message of an angel
you revealed to us the incarnation of your Son;
now, through his suffering and death
lead us to the glory of his resurrection.
We ask this through Christ our Lord.

R. Amen.

139

Acknowledgments

The prayers in this book were selected from many wonderful prayers, nearly 700 of them, submitted to the Daughters of St. Paul through schools, religious education programs, and families in Canada and the United States. In order to protect the privacy of the authors, we are not able to list individual contributors here, but our warmest thanks go to the following principals, religious education directors, teachers, and parents, whose participation made this project possible—and most of all, to the special young Catholics whose prayers brought it to life.

Cardinal Joseph Bernadin School, Orland Hills, Illinois—Ms. Pahl, Ms. Kristin, Mrs. Geary, Ms. McBride, Mrs. Lawton, Mrs. McLaughlin, Mrs. Sluis, Mrs. Gutrich, Ms. Roy, Mrs. O'Neill, Mrs. Ballantine

Ascension Catholic School, Oak Park, Illinois—Mrs. Johnson

Brockman Family, Wisconsin Rapids, Wisconsin—Mrs. Brockman

Buonocore Family, Vestavia Hills, Alabama—
Mrs. Buonocore

Catholic Community of Lexington, Lexington,
Massachusetts—Mrs. Rosa, Ms. Lowry, Ms.
McLaughlin

Church of the Blessed Sacrament
Religious Education Program, Walpole,
Massachusetts—Mr. Dittrich

Cordes Family, Yucca Valley, California—Mrs.
Cordes

Holy Rosary Academy, Anchorage, Alaska—
Ms. Kinney

Notre Dame Academy, Staten Island, New
York—Ms. Meador, Mrs. Stanislaro, Mrs.
Brown, Mrs. Holiday, Mrs. Signorelli, Mrs.
Gibbons, Mrs. Ficchi

St. Anastasia School, Waukegan, Illinois—Mrs.
Brisbois

St. Anne Catholic Family School, Saratoga
Springs, Utah—Mrs. Gilson

St. Bede School, Hayward, California—Ms.
Waffle, Ms. Garcia, Mr. Ian Leary

St. Clare Catholic School, Woodbridge,
Ontario—Ms. DiVincenzo, Mr. Roberto, Ms.
Santangelo

St. Cornelius School, Chicago, Illinois—Mrs. Szlak-Aimone

St. Francis Cathedral School, Metuchen, New Jersey—Mrs. Freeman, Mrs. Major

St. Helena School, Edison, New Jersey—Ms. Saltys, Ms. Garland, Mrs. Ur, Ms. Ericksen

St. Mary's Catholic School, Alexandria, Virginia—Mrs. Mears, Mrs. Burroughs, Mrs. Kennedy

St. Matthew School, Edison, New Jersey—Miss Fiore, Ms. Duarte, Mrs. Muscolino

St. Pius School, Redwood City, California—Mrs. Armando, Mrs. Grund, Miss Leitch

St. Rita School, Alexandria, Virginia—Mrs. Manaker

Tibbetts Family, Sioux Falls, South Dakota—Mr. Tibbetts

Villarreal Family, Round Rock, Texas—Mrs. Villarreal

Who are the Daughters of St. Paul?

We are Catholic sisters. Our mission is to be like Saint Paul and tell everyone about Jesus! There are so many ways for people to communicate with each other. We want to use all of them so everyone will know how much God loves us. We do this by printing books (you're holding one!), making radio shows, singing, helping people at our bookstores, using the Internet, and in many other ways.

Visit our Web site at www.pauline.org

Pauline
BOOKS & MEDIA

The Daughters of St. Paul operate book and media centers
at the following addresses. Visit, call or write the one
nearest you today, or find us on the World Wide Web,
www.pauline.org

CALIFORNIA
3908 Sepulveda Blvd,
Culver City, CA 90230
310-397-8676

2640 Broadway Street,
Redwood City, CA 94063
650-369-4230

5945 Balboa Avenue,
San Diego, CA 92111
858-565-9181

FLORIDA
145 S.W. 107th Avenue,
Miami, FL 33174
305-559-6715

HAWAII
1143 Bishop Street, Honolulu,
HI 96813   808-521-2731

Neighbor Islands call:
866-521-2731

ILLINOIS
172 North Michigan
Avenue, Chicago, IL 60601
312-346-4228

LOUISIANA
4403 Veterans Memorial
Blvd, Metairie, LA 70006
504-887-7631

MASSACHUSETTS
885 Providence Hwy,
Dedham, MA 02026
781-326-5385

MISSOURI
9804 Watson Road,
St. Louis, MO 63126
314-965-3512

NEW JERSEY
561 U.S. Route 1, Wick
Plaza, Edison, NJ 08817
732-572-1200

NEW YORK
150 East 52nd Street,
New York, NY 10022
212-754-1110

PENNSYLVANIA
9171-A Roosevelt Blvd,
Philadelphia, PA 19114
215-676-9494

SOUTH CAROLINA
243 King Street, Charleston,
SC 29401
843-577-0175

TENNESSEE
4811 Poplar Avenue,
Memphis, TN 38117
901-761-2987

TEXAS
114 Main Plaza, San
Antonio, TX 78205
210-224-8101

VIRGINIA
1025 King Street,
Alexandria, VA 22314
703-549-3806

CANADA
3022 Dufferin Street,
Toronto, ON M6B 3T5
416-781-9131